CRACKED FLUTES

Blues from the Soul - Poems

CRACKED FLUTES

Blues from the Soul - Poems

Vol. 2

OBED LADINY

Copyright 2019 by Obed Ladiny

All rights reserved.
Printed in the United States of America.

No part of this book may be reproduced in any form or by any electronic means, including information storage and retrieval systems, without permission in writing from the publisher or author, except by a reviewer, who may quote brief passages in a review.

Published August 20, 2019

ISBN: 978-1-7331995-6-8 (Paperback)
ISBN: 978-1-7331995-7-5 (eBook)

*"The human capacity for burden is like bamboo—
far more flexible than you'd ever believe at first glance."*

—Jodi Picoult, My Sister's Keeper

Contents

one

Birds Inside

What's goin on in there?
Let 'em loose.
Spill, splash, dash.
Let 'em be seen,
heard, touched.
Give 'em a scent
however you like.
Don't let 'em waste
or evaporate
without anyone else
having met 'em.
Utter nonsense, intangible?
Not worthy of a room
to call their own,
or a sheet to spread themselves
unabashedly
skipping and spinning
like ballerinas
dancing before you?
Give 'em faces,
arms and legs;
make 'em sit, stand,
walk or run.
Speak 'em forth!
Let 'em fly

Dry Trees

Sea of peoples,
imagine our groan

dry trees, orphans'
dusted feet

in red-hot sands
due for the rain.

Mom & Work

You let your hair down,
and your nails were glossed.
No, it wasn't your birthday
or any other special occasion
as I remember it.
The white cotton skirt with red dots
clung to you, unlike the usual
loosed jean pants.
I sat on the passenger side
of the four-door, gray, Toyota
and observed your callous fingers
on the steering wheel.
The sacks below your eyes
revealed to me what life was doing to you.
I don't remember whether
we were coming home or going somewhere,
but I do recall this moment
in the chapters of those long
humid slaving years you had.
I was a son relieved to see
a little variance on you.

Reunion at Mama's

Horses came running on fire,
but the evening did sing.
A time to be written on walls.
No more spiders creeping in our attics.
No more bed bugs making holes in our brains.
May Niagara invigorate our neurons,
so we rise from pits
of spiritually frozen bodies
to sunlight. At the dinner table:

a fat roast turkey,
rice, red beans, mash potatoes, lasagnas,
salads, and sesame breads—turn bellies
to balloons. Hyena laughter join forks
and spoons clanking on large saucers
over rolling eyes with delight
and pierced eye peas. The black years

and our inner spiders went hiding tonight.
This victory proves inner power.
Let innocence move back
into our membrane upstairs.
May the fires of our will
burn old documented leaves
filed within our heads,
invaded with insects and roaches,
mildews and dung, wrenches, hammers,
and knives—all down a cliff
into a gleaming sea. The horses
came running on fire,
but the evening did sing.

Brothers

what if
  i didn't buy the plane ticket?
left florida   for new york.

i remember   bruno.
  taylor.   rony.
all grown now.   doing cart

wheels on the lawn.
  catching a football. jumping
on the bed.   wrestling.

broken arm. smashed mirror.
  used to be the four of us.
little boys then.   and mother.

now scattered
  adults. north carolina, florida
new york.

Those Young Days When We Saved the World

Fingers hold the square controller.
Blushed thumbs at the tip
press against two round red buttons
and dark gray compass arrows.

Living room darkens.
Afternoon turns into midnight unawares.

Tinges of pain and numbness at each
thumb's tip.

We morphed into the good guys
with a mission script: save the planet.

Little brother—partner
against evil—many nights like this
we went to bed losers,

not tonight. We came this far to finality,
dejection not an option, even if
our thumbs cry out with redness.

Let's save the girl, the world, and our dignity.

Resurrecting Mama's Dish

I once sat
in the boat,

held up
the prize

hanging from
a hook

before
dark.

Pages
turn

like
waves,

showing
a

school
of dish.

Crisp edge
of leaflets

damp
and drying

on the
counter.

Spinach
and saltfish,

on the side—green
and purple grapes

line on
the saucer

like
necklace beads.

Flour
and olive oil,

strips of yellow
and red pepper,

onions and
tomatoes—

tantalize
between the pages

of
yesterday.

The flesh
sizzles

from
the pan,

the round eyes
and scales;

limes float
in a water pot

of extracted
inedible remains

is how she
used to make it.

My nose
reassures me—

*you're doing
fine baby,*

*you're doing
fine.*

On Returning to the City

After three months in Memphis, Tennessee,
I'm back in Manhattan—this borough
survived without me.

The Greyhound bus pants like a tired dog,
turning corners between parked cars
in the early morning.

This time, the Apple didn't run and hide
to pencil the eyebrows
and put on make-up and lipstick for me.

In the cold, a bearded black man,
shivering and determined, sticks out
his palm, talks to drivers at the stop light.

From inside the Greyhound
I survey streets and dead ends, graffiti on walls,
looking deep for signs of ardor.

Doesn't she know that I've come to surprise her?

March 2017

The Beat of N.Y.C

       Can't be slow
walking through
       the revolving door.
It's like dance,
       gotta keep in step,
or a jump rope,
       gotta jump in
at the right time,
       or you'll stop the flow
of the spinning rope.
       Nobody›s smiling
about mis-steps
       and two left feet. Gotta
learn the rhythm.

The Light on Each Face

Took them to Prospect Park,
sat on a bench next to swings,
watched their little faces glow
as they ran around the playground
and quickly made friends.

The youngest of the three, full of life.
Her omnipresence is a reminder
that Planet Fitness has a good deal
posted on its glass doors for me.

Daddy! daddy! Let's play hide-and-seek.
Can't hide from me but she'll try.
Ah, why not if it makes her little heart
happy, she'll be Little Red Riding Hood,
I'll be the big bad wolf.

Ice cream vendor, predictably convenient.
I came ready. They'll eat today,
oh they'll eat. Food will come out their noses.

Next stop Prospect Zoo, the least I can do.
Let's greet mid-April with photos of flowers
blooming pink and lovely this afternoon.

Rent payment will be put on hold for two weeks,
that new Mac at Best Buy can wait,
new suit at the men's store is going nowhere,
and the chores will never end.

two

They Say Fathers Are Never Around

They say fathers are never around
& the month of June is a needle
against the skin of statistics.

They say the boys wear dresses now
& never get old.

The girls wear pants
& look beyond their years.

Their distant fathers have less ingenious ways
of combing through old stories
for any sort of self-vindication.

Some fathers are indeed losers & devils.
Some fathers are victims of witches
& some fathers give up dignity
through suffering

for the sanity
of their innocent bystander
off-springs. These fathers hold-on til

their last breath
like captains willing to go down
with their ship
in times of great distress.

& just maybe many we know to have jumped ship
were thrown off

against their will, if we could only be flies
in those ships before they sunk.

Mars Men Sailing on Venus Shores

Alright, men!
we've more questions now
than when we first began—

but that's fine as we explore.
it suffices to say,
we're sailing on an exotic shore.

Stumbling Upon Gold

Love.

Some say it's a long kiss.
Some say—steamy passions.
Maybe diamond gifts.
Some show it with a batch of flowers on one's doorstep.
Some believe it's a time out in the moonlight.
It seems to be there when giggling together
till the bellies ache.
Other say, it's the sparkles that compete in their eyes.
Some say, it's the aura of the moment. Others say—no,
it's a delightful head rush in an amusement park.
A man says—it's a full belly by her magic hands.
A woman says—security from the greens in his wallet.
Someone else says—a dream home and life of luxury.
Another interjects—children as gifts!

All these are from lovers, I suppose.

May I interpose another face?

Could it not be called patience?
How long does it linger with meager means?
Is it a chess board with prize as pawn?
How bright does it shine at flaws?
Will it be stronger in the days of sickness?
Can it be trusted in the hours of absence?
Will it hold on in unexpected turbulent weather?
Can it be deluded by greener grass?

What if the wine lately lacks fermentation?
And the song off-key?

Those who remain with you in the latter are rare.
They are warm treasure souls in this world of cold.
Finding this soul is finding more than gold.

Roses & Thorns

Do roses have thorns?
Can they prick and drip blood too?
They're a variety of colors
with scents of almost heaven,
so inviting,
irresistible.

Don't be astonished when
you discover a hidden thorn
that pierces your skin
within your gorgeous rose.
Will you then understand
that they carry thorns?

Should you swear
to never hold one again?
Should you avoid them altogether
since they have thorns?

How best to handle them?

Dancing Flames

We remember how they held each other—
like two Jellyfish
in the bottom of the ocean.

Passionate to a degree, hard to put into words.
Theirs were the playful tongues and the spittle,
which danced at all hours
by slow, gentle imaginary tunes.

How silly they were to shine
with the constellations.
Their past is bottled up in each one's
Dream chamber of memories.

Dances of the flames—
the lost art that slipped, sneaked, and hid.
Like a cruel joker it did!

The turbulent tides
dropped like drumbeats upon their lives
and left them torn and stranded.

The whereabouts of their sacred fire?
It's there—we just know,
or is it extinguished to nevermore
in its symphony fill the air?

A Spectrum of Romeos & Juliets

Aren't we lucky to come across
quiet mushrooms
of Pearl Harbors
with much dark history
swirling inside?

& some hearts are broken glass—
you draw near to bleed

you hold bouquets
with visions of heaven
like a soldier welcoming friendly fire

To the Person in the Mirror

what a world this is.
where are you in it
and when did you leave?

you say your world
is made of steel
and I ask about the clouds of graces
to which you pause
as if looking for words of mercy.

your smile,
your chuckle earlier
troubles me
when I consider the fact
their jokes at the gathering
wasn't even funny.

everything
will be alright.
one day you won't
have to pretend
to laugh in order to convince
them or yourself
that you're not a ghost.

it isn't you alone.
you're in great company.
and yes, you're not in a dream.
yes, you've joined the sad statistics of
the crushed and tossed. and yes
of course you're valuable.
you're valuable.
you're valuable.
you know that.

Coffee & Podcasts

these days
these nights
a hammer pounds against my head
after each death in your sea

my tongue is sour
neck & back needs untwisting
no matter how early
or late i close my eyes

you pinned me down   yeah
less of you   i'm no floating stone
too much of you   still   i'm no floating stone

was i gone too early or too late
with the lights on
and a Tony Robbins' book on the floor
beside the bed
or its pages folded under my back again?

these days
these nights
a hammer pounds against my head
before i sit up
& command my brain
to hit the shower

then get dressed
meet the front door

guru podcasts
plugged into my ears

as I walk in the morning dew air
with stars fading in the fog

along with a coffee in my hand
from the corner store

to undo what you have done again
and again

till i won't need these
in the mornings

& i won't need these
in the evenings

three

This Gift of Knowing

Someday I'll go to bed, won't need
an alarm clock for the morning
to sit up, get ready for work,
and run to the screeching train.

No looking at my watch
between hours
while on the job,
no need for weekends

or a paycheck that won't sit
in the bank, but comes through a door
every other week and leaves
through another for necessities.

No more tv, newspapers,
or hearing my own voice.
No more light, cable, gas bill,
monthly rent, blah, blah, blah, blah, blah...

Hopes, goals, and fears
won't matter.
One day, I'll lay down
and won't even know I was a sleep

like we've all been doing
since birth each time we lay to rest, except that day
all will have been over, when I finally
know I was gone.

Back on the Road

i write a to-do list
the same one from last week.

this time i'm adding—
rise earlier than 6am,
exhilarate or vomit in a daily journal,
exercise,
meditate,
avoid trigger books,
trigger places,
trigger people,
trigger social media pages,
trigger this trigger that

i hope to God—time
destroys all triggers & every ounce
of lava in the heart
of this toilet paper.

how do you un-flush,
un-wet,
& unentangle?

many say—one list after the next,
one foot before the other,
one crossed-out accomplishment
gets sweeter & sweeter.

To My Daughters

Your voice over the phone
force my lips to stretch
revealing teeth long since hidden
behind the shades
of my mouth.

Your "Hello, Daddy!"
is daylight
entering a dark room
filled with dusts and cobwebs.

My ears are attentive
to every sound that formulates
words you utter across
the line like a desert nomad
finds oasis in a journey.

The wings inside of me flutter,
and I think of when and how
to reach and fulfill the days
I've promised. I sense a silent,
almost secret flutter inside you.

So I wish you'll invoke and hold
to the Power, who is greater than
our fleeting breath. As long as
you remember this, I shouldn't fear
to embrace the falling of dusk.

Last Night They Came for Aunty

1.
She was sick in bed again.
Their shadows
roamed near the candle-light
on the limestone floor.
Noise in her room?
They came for aunty.
She's no better today.

2.
Your name's written on the outside
wall of your house.
He's coming tonight. The moon
crouches over Port-au-Prince.
Ooh! Ooh! You better wipe it off.
He's coming for you, tonight.
He'll eat you alive.

3.
Turn the page, turn the page. The name.
What name?
That name!
S.a.t.a.n?
He said it! He said it!
I didn't mean to.
Shhh! Turn the page.

4.
Dad gets off bed,
and quickly lights the oil lamp.
We hear what he hears.

Shadows circling round
making every hair stand.
He grabs the Bible.
Noise augments.
He turns it to Psalm 91 and reads,
then picks up the songbook
to sing a hymn.

All quiet now.

Far Country

...the younger son...took his journey into a far country,
and there wasted his substance with riotous living.
–Luke 15:13 Holy Bible

Tired of the minimum wage.
Tired of these stinking clothes.
Tired of patching holes in my shoes.
Tired of those blinking neon lights
and half naked women billboards
down these circuit streets.
Tired of parking meters on almost every block.
Tired of the annual costs hikes.
Tired of that fat belly, cigarette smoking boss.
Tired of my parasitic "friends".
Tired of bunnies draining my pockets.
Tired of this half full liquor bottle.
Tired of being tired.

My old man was rich and wise.
Even his butlers had it better.
I'll go to him, beg to be one of them
or fall on my knees
and ask to stop by now and then
for crumbs,
dry fish bones,
saucy red beans and tomatoes
that fall to the dogs from his table.
Anything from back home,
anything but
this far country.

Life's a Bully

how you slither

        around my mind for neck and breath

how you roar

        at my face so the heart trembles

how you claw

        my money and dreams then fly away

how you charge

        with your horns, nostrils in smoke

how you move

        in the ring for the knockout

how i keep

        coming   back

Dreadful Journey

hello dreadful journey
here i am in your face
like a little bird
caught in your palms
    you old rugged road.

got me where
you want me—trapped,
secluded in the mud
of emotions. drained.
i'm at your mercy
    you old rugged road.

this isn't the neighborhood.
this isn't the house I saw.
this isn't the love anticipated.
this isn't the body.
this isn't the hairs i wanted on my head.
this isn't the me i wanted to stare back at.

each day is the same
and i'm at your mercy
    you old rugged road.

i'm fuming in your grips
and i'm no longer afraid of
your mighty hold.
go ahead crush me.
i'm not afraid, and nor do i care.
crush me. did you think
i would beg like before?
i've gotten stronger and bolder
in the midst of your prison.

Remove the Stone

These four walls are constrictors.
I'd like to sit on the back-breaking mattress
for hours, but want a long life
which the walls will only snuff
with each coming day
till I'm gone.
The miserable dusty fan whined
last night
till it died while I slept.

I sit on the edge
of this squeaky bed, still,
and adjusting my eyes
to the dark
warm windowless space.
Clock's red lights – 5:09am.
Still early.
I'll lay down
and wait
for the breakfast shop
three blocks away to open.
Going out is a must, anywhere
towards life and movements.
Returning here later
will feel just right—away
from the heart of the world.

The Soldier in You

the soldier in you
might flicker
in the wind and dark

your flame
that salted the world
with your old spirit   sways in the gloom

the night is immense

but push your rays
against the jealous pitch thirsty
for your spark   wanting you
extinguished

for you this time   for you alone
be glad
be glad

After the Fire

When the house was burning
for many years
& each of our lives were at stake,
long time friends I often hung out with
stood at their front doors
across the streets---sipping on kool-aid,
watching the flames.

Many months later, on some accidental brush---
some said, 'hey, how's life?
We miss the old days since you moved.
How about meeting with one another
for old times sake to catch up
on current news of our lives?'

I smiled with a glint in my eyes
and said, 'cept for some loss
and affected lives, all's well dear friends.
You have no idea how I miss you too.
how's your families & children? How's
the old churches in the community goin?
Been awhile for sure. You're right, we
could gather like old times.'

four

Remainders in the Division

a body to revive
           a name to engrave

these muscles to exhaust
           footprints to retrace

soil for a seed
       ᴄnough sky for a tree

Postmodern Rumors on God

He has become a big secret
hiding like dust particles
under: door mats,
fingerprints.

He's a rabbit foot,
chained crosses,
ritual icons on living room walls.

He's an admired museum,
an occasional opium

And we?

Drunks,
unable to get out of bed early,
unwilling to be fascinated for an hour
with trees and clouds,

afraid they can sing.

Fuels

They say it's the end,
I say
a new beginning,
my heart
thumps
with life's rhythm.

I'm prepared
to fight
and run
its marathon.

There's oil
in my feet,
wings
in my arms.

Ambition,
like children
runs and plays
in my brain.

They'll soon learn
not to count me out.
They'll soon know
what their words
have done.

The Late Student

it is warming and crowded in my head
on a cool spring night of stillness.
i hear my thoughts as the ink
bleeds and dries upon the leaf.

miles in coming to release
from the thousand voices of wonder
as to when this heaping will cease
and the books lay closed next to my pen.

rehearsing my journey's end as I labor
through this tunnel of loading volumes,
my joy, my grin before me view
a celebration in a gown of excellence –

the husband standing stately.
father with children in the midst
of black robes, caps, and yellow stripes.
imagine me elated and relieved.

recompensed for quarters and quarters
of exhaustion in mind on a wooden chair
with pains and labor to produce my station,
while pages, long hand and short hand turn.

seems like deja vu nights of spring.
the same repeats itself upon me,
the dream a distant journey – far-off lights
forever delaying to brighten my path.

Creeping Sunset

you
want to do
what you
used to do
thinking you
will
and discover
that you can't keep up
walking or running
with the young men
up the hilly Bronx,
heart beats
knee spring
squeaks
like rusty coils
from an old
car needing new
parts, tune-ups,
and oil.
don't forget
mileage used
on those joints
and feet. you're
surprised to see
how age
crept in,
the mind
the last
to know,
informed

by
the body
  ---you can't
    stay up no more
      in the late hours

The Last Hymn

In control
while everyone cries.
Give them tissues.
Tell them
where to sit.

The family needs a man
to stand in your stead.

But when they sing
my childhood song
you used to play
on a radio
back then
in that old house,
all the years come back

to shake my lips and elbows.

The Sky

The sky isn't blue
and the clouds aren't white or grey
as I once knew them.
The chapters of a life
can be compared to missing pages
or loose leaves disordered within a book.
I can either see it all for what it is and be brave,
or crumble under the weight of this giant stone
proving to us that not all mirrors are accurate,
and if they are,
not all eyes looking deep have seen human nature
as it is;
otherwise, our wit, vision, and consumption of red pills
would have produced an impenetrable fortress
against the all-predictable fluctuating tides.

Tomorrow I'll Go to Bed Early

Cab driver talks.
I agree
and look at passing street names.
He asks where I'm from.
I tell him.
Says he's from the west indies.
He asks about occupation.
I tell him.
"Great, but plenty of people do it
only for the money" he says.

Are we moving faster than the Q train? I ask.

"Greedy whites trying to take over,
opening shops in our neighborhoods", he says.
I smile, look at passing street names.
He complains car ahead caused him
to yield to the red. I look at minutes
and squint at yellow lanes.
"That guy on the left must be Chinese
by the way he swerves. His eyes
too narrow to see the road", he says.

"How close are we?" I ask.

"Don't worry.
Can you tell me how to get there
from this highway?" He asks.

I shout streets from my phone's GPS.

Give him bills.
He has no change.

I watch the seconds.

He searches his dashboard and curses.

I stare at my workplace.

He curses his pockets and searches.

Incoming Envelopes

piled on the kitchen table
unheeded,
kept from the trash bin.
I'll slash one through
maybe tomorrow,
a week or a month from now,
eventually the senders
will hear from me.
Not avoiding anyone
or unconcerned,
too busy these days
trying to keep sane.
I swim above their voices
like a fugitive
till I should turn myself in,
arms forward for handcuffs
of signatures, dates, and promises.

Message to Grim Reaper

Give me time
to find the word,
to form a sentence,

for the churning
in my belly
and the rock in my throat

to shrink.

Another Day

It's September. The sound
of fire-crackers in July
comes from outside my window.
Three quick successive explosions
derail my train of thought
as I lie in bed in mid-day.
I imagine somewhere out there—
sirens, red concrete, yellow NO CROSSING tapes,
and onlookers.
Night maybe closing in somewhere
not too far inside the head of someone
as I lie here awake unready to get up.

The Peaceful-Cruel Day

I wonder about the clock between my lungs,
but imagine life – a thick book, with many chapters
to go. Sometimes my bones bring to mind
heavy classic tomes with white pages
turned yellow, when getting out of bed
or walking and panting up a flight of stairs.

Yeah, I know. I can't stop it, and we don't know
when the day, the big day, the peaceful but cruel
day (which to most is like the merging of dark
clouds) will come. The one that punches us
in the gut. The one that overwhelms us
into silence. The one that makes each day,
month, and year – reflective sign-posts
before and after its arrival.

The Twinkling of an Eye

At the twinkling of an eye
I was born.

At the twinkling of an eye
I was talking.

Celebrated many of my birthdays.

Right and wrong wasn't always clear.

Went to Malcolm Elementary;
there, I once battled with a bully
as my little brother Ro stood by anxious.
Me and the bully tossed and rolled on the school's grass.
My brother hoped that bullies eat dirt,
and that I'd be the victor in the nightmare.
Once again interrupted by the bell
and the shouting of teachers.
All the cheerleaders scattered like pigeons.

Mother used to carry me
from the living room couch
and put me to bed,
while in my dreams
I was in captain Kirk's ship of Star Trek
in another adventure.

At the twinkling of an eye
went to Nova High.
In those days
many boys wrote letters
to the girls they admire
and sent them with perfume.

At the twinkling of an eye
jumped through fads.
Thought it was all cool.
The end of the world
was about the latest jacket, jeans, or shoes.
Give me some friends
Styles and name brands.
Pass me the ball, Jordan.
Where's my drawing pad?
Favorite rap song is playing.
Blast that radio. Turn it up.

Mom, leave me to myself.
I'm fine.
Keep your strange songs
and your Sunday school lessons
at a distance.
Mom, relax!
You're being uptight for no reason.
I'm no child can't you see?

At the twinkling of an eye
had my first job at a fast-food.

At the twinkling of an eye
ran away
like an underground slave
from mom's iron grip.

Many blinks later—
packed my things for New York.
Goodbye Florida!
Here at last.

New circumstances.

I found or salvation found me.
It was special.
Jesus voice.
A whisper.
Grew loud as a trumpet's.
The LORD called me to His mountain top.
I followed the voice.
Later, I came down with a glory face.

At the twinkling of an eye
worked with my own hands,
paid rent for a room,
learned to give my dues,
earned my plate,
and washed my own wear.
Independence
has never been so sweet.
Yet

I became bitter. Home-sick.

At the twinkling of an eye
we met at church.
At the twinkling of an eye
We signed the book.
We were locked
and exchanged promises
to throw away the keys.

At the twinkling of an eye
Came the first,
the second,
and the third daughter.

At the twinkling of an eye

it really dawned—
life has begun
and all that comes with it.
It can be a flower
or a concrete
or both.

You're a man now, I tell myself.
Not a boy.
Tighten your belt
is the cliché.
Reminds me of Langston's poem
where the mother said, "Son,
life has been no crystal stairs."
For sure, life is a strange creature.
But sometimes I wonder
if it's just the other way around.
I must be an anvil for me
and the ones I love
and cannot imagine ever living without.

And now I fear to blink an eye,
for if I do
they'll soon grow up.
I'll soon turn gray.
If only I can blink an eye
and be young again.
Young again.
No place like home.
Young again.

At what cost? At what loss?

Maybe I can revisit
old chapters and settings.

Ghost towns of the past.
Maybe like an angel
on a mission
righting all wrongs.

At what cost? At what loss?

I have this anchoring hope
from the promise
told me from the mountain:
that at the twinkling of an eye
we will all be changed.
We will all be changed.

In the Heart of the Earth

An armor-clad soldier
Casts dice to the ground.
Five other soldiers lose
The portion. He takes the cloth
As his own, then lifts his eyes

Toward three men nailed
Hands and feet, stretched naked
On stakes, lifting
Themselves up for breath.
Black crows fly back
And forth near the hill.

The one they crowned king,
Whose bones from his chest
Protrude and body bloodied, looks up
Towards the dark sky at midday,
And utters: *Eloi, Eloi, lama sabachthani?*
Observers walk away singly
And in companies—eyes

To the ground. Thick clouds
Gather over Golgotha. A handful
Remain with the soldiers looking on
As the one crowned king rests his
Head, shuts his eyes.

This Side of Life

There You are stretched nude on a tree.
Here I am hiding from a world peeking at me.
I feel that I've done nothing deserving of
being naked. How dare I compare
this uneasiness of mine to your vulnerable body
against sunlight, clouds, multitudes, and crows.
Seems like no one gets to the other side
without some mud.

"Do not judge me by my success, judge by how many times I fell down and got back up again."

—Nelson Mandela

To the Reader

It means a lot to me that you purchased Cracked Flutes: Blues from the Soul – Poems, volume 2. You could have picked any other book to read, but you chose this one. I am grateful!

If you enjoyed this poetry book and found some benefit in reading it, I'd like to hear from you and hope that you could take some time to post a review on the platform you purchased it or whichever platform you prefer to inform others of your discovery. Thank you.

About the Author

OBED LADINY is an educator and a frequent participant in literature and poetry forums. He enjoys writing contemporary free-verse poems that deal with society, relationships, places, history, religion, and opinionated epiphanies from reflections on various topics. Some of his poems first appeared in *TWJ Magazine, the Poems-For-All Project, In Between Hangovers, Red Fez, and Torrid Literature Journal.* Ladiny is a native of Haiti, raised in Ft. Lauderdale, Florida and later became a resident of New York.

My Thoughts for Today

My Thoughts for Today

My Thoughts for Today

_____

_____

_____

_____

_____

_____

_____

_____

_____

_____

_____

_____

_____

_____

_____

_____

_____

_____

_____

_____

_____

_____

My Thoughts for Today

My Thoughts for Today

My Thoughts for Today

My Thoughts for Today

My Thoughts for Today

My Thoughts for Today

_____

_____

_____

_____

_____

_____

_____

_____

_____

_____

_____

_____

_____

_____

_____

_____

_____

_____

_____

_____

_____

My Thoughts for Today

My Thoughts for Today

My Thoughts for Today

My Thoughts for Today

My Thoughts for Today

My Thoughts for Today

My Thoughts for Today

_____

_____

_____

_____

_____

_____

_____

_____

_____

_____

_____

_____

_____

_____

_____

_____

_____

_____

_____

_____

My Thoughts for Today

My Thoughts for Today

My Thoughts for Today

My Thoughts for Today

My Thoughts for Today

My Thoughts for Today

My Thoughts for Today

My Thoughts for Today

My Thoughts for Today

_____

_____

_____

_____

_____

_____

_____

_____

_____

_____

_____

_____

_____

_____

_____

_____

_____

_____

_____

_____

My Thoughts for Today

My Thoughts for Today

My Thoughts for Today

Also by Obed Ladiny

One Flesh - Poems
Cracked Flutes: Blues from the Soul – Poems, Volume 1

Made in the USA
Middletown, DE
27 February 2023

25805030R00066